This book belongs to

_____

ABC

with Winnie-the-Pooh

Illustrated by E. H. Shepard

A a apple

Bb balloon

Cc Christopher Robin

Dd door

Ee Eeyore

F f friends

Gg gate

Hh honey

I i island

J j jump

K k Kanga

L l letters

Mm mirror

Nn North Pole

Oo Owl

P p Piglet

Qq quilt

Rr Rabbit

Ss snow

T t Tigger

Uu umbrella

V v violets

Ww

Winnie-the-Pooh

Xx expotition

Yy yawn

Zz buzzing bees

EGMONT
We bring stories to life

First published in Great Britain 2005
by Egmont Books Limited
239 Kensington High Street, London W8 6SA
Based on the "Winnie-the-Pooh" works
Copyright A.A. Milne and E.H. Shepard
Colouring of the illustrations © 1970, 1973 and 1974 E.H. Shepard and Egmont Books Limited
This edition © 2005 Disney Enterprises, Inc

ISBN 1 4052 1842 8
1 3 5 7 9 10 8 6 4 2
Printed in Singapore